JOEL SHAPIRO

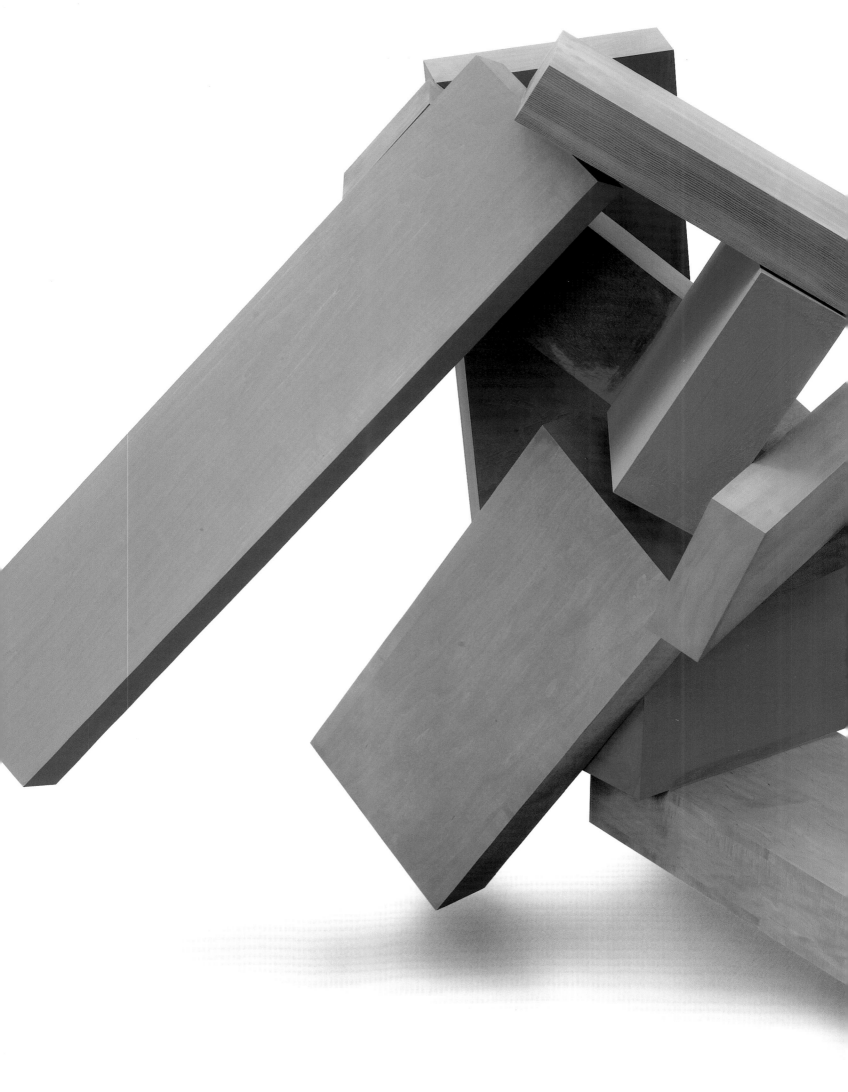

JOEL SHAPIRO

NEW SCULPTURE   NOVEMBER 2, 2007–JANUARY 19, 2008

PACEWILDENSTEIN

545 WEST 22ND STREET NEW YORK NY 10011

PENDING

Richard Shiff

Figuration skewed

Criticism is discriminating. If there is an art to what critics do, it is the art of establishing differences and distinctions. Recently, the situation has been complicated by the practice of distinguishing works according to their effect on familiar distinctions. This is not to suggest that critics have turned inward, criticizing their own practice. Instead, their concern is whether the work of art undermines hierarchical distinctions (a good thing) or preserves them (not so good, it seems). Many critics praise works for subverting oppositions that bear a moral force in the culture. Presumably, the society will change if its members can no longer distinguish between public and private, elite and popular, unique and repeating, same and different, female and male, self and other.[1] The list could be continued, but something is amiss. We are growing short on fixed cultural identities and rigid conceptual oppositions to unhinge, ironize, and subvert. The strategy itself, having become a conventional value in art, has lost its edge, its critical significance.

In this environment, where do we locate Joel Shapiro's sculpture? Does it undermine anything? It might seem that Shapiro has been pursuing the most central distinction for modern artists—the separation of representation from abstraction—and eliminating it. His works seem to hover on the edge of representation and abstraction, subverting the distinction. (Here, any number of analogously equivocating metaphors could replace "hover on the edge.") Although by no means incorrect, this kind of observation proves pointless. It introduces a guiding opposition—representation versus abstraction—only to deny it, without identifying the ground of the initial difference, some crucial characteristic that would belong to only one member of the antithetical pair, and not the other. The degree of qualification introduced by the metaphor—hovering on the edge—suggests that the opposition may have been false from the start, false at least in Shapiro's case, because it nowhere holds up. The availability of a conceptual antithesis tempts a critic to invoke it, if only to

demonstrate its subversion, telling a good story along the way. But for Shapiro, experience outweighs concepts. He is unlikely to regard representation and abstraction as truly distinct realms of activity: "All the intellectualizing one does ... and the critical input ... When you're working you don't even think about it. You're just sticking (the sculpture) together."[2]

A shift in terminology would be useful: Shapiro's sculptures are figurative. Representation does not define them; abstraction does not define them. Instead, the sculptures "figure" the artist's internalized experience, both sensory and emotional. In several respects, this experience extends beyond the immediate presence and moment of the sculptural object. Representation, which Shapiro associates with depiction or illustration, is not his issue. "I was never interested in representational imagery, doing a portrait or a full figure," he stated in 1990; "I (have been) much more interested ... in the psychology of the form."[3] Was he suggesting that "psychology" is more abstract than representational? The notion is sensible, but the verbal opposition (representation versus abstraction) hardly helps matters. "In the end," he now says, "all work regardless of how abstract is referential. ... All work has figurative reference."[4] Like words suggesting words, any form suggests some other form, eventually returning even the most fantastic of inventions to a familiar, "real" world.

A related pronouncement secures this notion: "Sculpture is always in the real world."[5] The materiality of sculpture adds substance to the figurative potential of a form. A work in three dimensions resembles other "real" things, at least slightly, by existing not only in the projective space of mental figuration but in a space experienced physically, which lends itself to figuration: "You can't refute (its) presence," Shapiro says.[6] "You" in this instance is your body (its sensations) and your mind (its imaginings), and both together (your emotions). Shapiro observes that the physical presence of sculpture allows a work at one moment to appear as a human figure and at the next as "a bunch of wood stuck together." He has referred to this as the difference between configuration (figuration integrating) and disfiguration (figuration disintegrating)—the directions are opposed but the process remains above all physical.[7]

The terminology of configuration and disfiguration (which Shapiro may have used only occasionally) has the advantage of avoiding the representation/abstraction dichotomy, a source of evaluative hierarchy. When critics present the history of modern art as a narrative, they commonly write of representational forms that gradually yield to abstract ones, a transition epitomized in the individual histories of, say, Piet

Mondrian, Jackson Pollock, and David Smith. For some writers, the advantage offered by abstraction would be an increased potential to realize personal, expressive intensity, since radical abstraction displaces the traditional stock of thematic clichés (no more picturesque scenes, no more allegories). Beyond abstraction, the history often continues with forms of art that isolate perceptual experience in a materialistic, quasi-architectural manner. Examples might be drawn from Donald Judd, Robert Irwin, Bridget Riley, Frank Stella, Robert Mangold, Richard Serra, and still others. If this is now a prevailing history of art, Shapiro's sculptural practice is historically skewed. His development is the solution to a different set of questions. His figuration is representational but also abstract; it is abstract but also representational. This observation is merely his beginning, not his end achievement. He never set about to demonstrate this theoretical and critical point, which for him quickly became a given.

Shapiro connects his art not only to the things of the world but to his own thoughts, his psychological disposition, his emotions. He once stated that "any abstract mark has something to do with ... being a person in the world." He might have said that abstraction itself is the representation of "being a person in the world," drawing abstraction and representation to the same close. Condensing this thought, he defined all markmaking as "implied figuration."[8] After the fact, he was hinting at a theory of the sculptor's indexical mark. He understood that all art, even if not representing anything else, would figure the emotional presence of the artist. Ironically, a theory of this sort would be of little use to an intuitive artist like Shapiro. It might be good for the critics, though—to help them make distinctions.

Into the air

What qualities are evident in the way that Shapiro configures his forms? Klaus Kertess notes both activity and restraint: the sculpture moves "into continuously shifting engagement with the viewer, but never overwhelms with superfluous mass and volume."[9] Shapiro himself stresses these points, but with different language: he wants his works to avoid any appearance of monumentality or the "colossal." To this end, he restricts the size of any single element. Large or small, his sculptural constructions divide into relatively manageable units of material, so that the character of a work is never the product of imposing size but rather of articulation. A Shapiro sculpture can seem to be all linkages, both taut and tenuous, with little solidifying volume. Its evocation of activity results from these linkages—"if the arm is moving, the

body is moving."[10] No component part is so fixed in place that the virtual movement of some other part fails to affect it. We associate this kind of sculptural articulation with living, integrated bodies.

Emotionally at least, an articulated body has more range than a monolithic mass of metal or a block of wood. Shapiro eliminates from his work any element or property he regards as adding extraneous spatial volume or gravitational mass. Such factors can deaden a lively configuration. To this end, he began to use relatively slight material components: "If (the work) sat on the ground, then somehow the perception of the piece was always limited by the architecture it was in. So I began to use sticks of wood to dislocate the mass into the air."[11] He applied his phrase "into the air" to particularly slender constructions of the late 1980s, but it is of more general relevance to the vitality of his sculpture.

"Into the air" is an apt metaphor for figurative abstractions that appear to pull up from a ground plane as much as they rest upon it. In this regard, untitled, 1987 (fig. 1) is not the most obvious example, but an interesting one. It presents a curious combination of possibilities also typical of Shapiro's more recent work: we can view this work as two sets of vertical elements leaning and even pressing against one another or, alternatively, as a single form rising, bending, and returning to the ground. Yet the same unitary structure seems to strain upward with a potential to lift itself from the ground by internal energy, as if it were a taut bow about to snap. The forms disregard gravity. We sense the effect as well in untitled, 2006–07 (pp. 24–25), despite its horizontal

fig. 1:
untitled, 1987, bronze, 48 3/8 x 51 1/4 x 34 1/4"

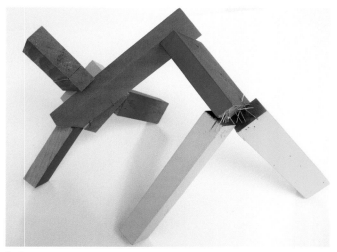

fig. 2:
Study for untitled, 2006–07 (pp. 24–25)

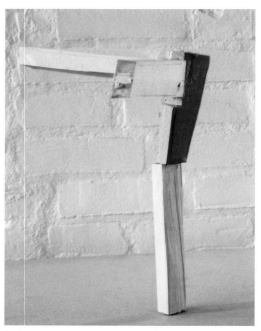

fig. 3:
Study for untitled, 2007 (p. 23)

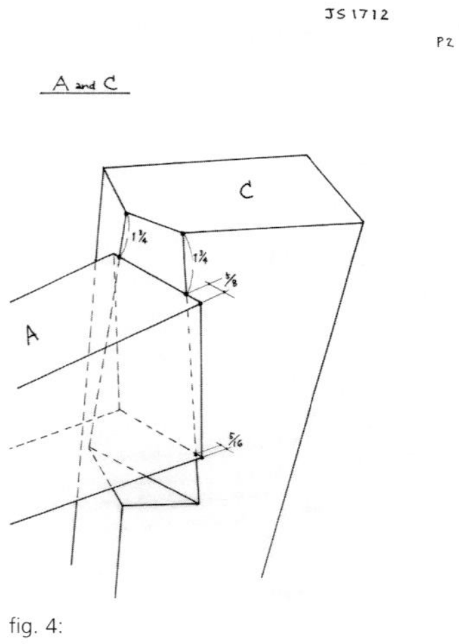

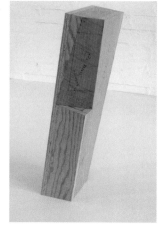

fig. 4:
Detail of a working drawing for the
fabrication of untitled, 2007 (p. 23)

fig. 5:
A wooden pattern for untitled, 2007 (p.23)

disposition and the blockiness of its elements. The form in its entirety seems remarkably light-footed, buoyant, and capable of rising. Shapiro's use of color—water-blasted paint, either rose or blue on selected elements, slight traces of yellow on some others—enhances the effect by dissociating the individual segments so that the blockiness of units does not become heavy by accumulation. This observation might hold for many of Shapiro's works: reason seems to tell us that they should appear heavier than they do. When we suspend reason, experience seizes the opportunity to correct it.

However metaphoric, Shapiro's "into the air" can be taken literally, because he typically begins a work with fragile constructions of narrow lengths of milled wood and studio scraps. These objects can be held in the hand and spatially reoriented at will (see the study for untitled, 2006–07; fig. 2). Quickly constructed, but subject to being pulled apart and readjusted over long periods of investigation, Shapiro's small studies are light enough in weight to support their internal connections no matter how they have been set to rest on the studio table. It may seem as if they float, gravity-free in the space of imagination. Many of the separate elements are initially regular and right-angled. Working with them, Shapiro cuts and recombines, either abutting or notching them to form joints at "capricious angles" (his term).[12] A relatively simple case of notching occurs in the study for untitled, 2007 (fig. 3; compare p. 23). This preliminary piece is straightforward, at least up to a point, since it has only four elements; but the planes of attachment become complicated because one surface is likely to extend ever so slightly beyond the other to which it connects. Typically, because of the eccentric joints, the distinct surface planes of a Shapiro sculpture become a mix of relatively broad and relatively narrow dimensions—a little bit of surface left exposed where two planes meet creates this kind of differentiation. To move from a study to a full-scale sculpture, the adventitious joints have to be mapped and engineered so that they remain rigid under a greatly increased gravitational pull. As part of the process, there may be studio drawings that record precise measurements (fig. 4); and works to be cast in metal require the fabrication of hollow patterns, constructed of planes of various kinds of wood, including industrial plywood (fig. 5). These have distinctive surface textures created by the use of power tools and saws of different gauges. Such textures transfer to the negative mold and finally to the poured, cast metal.

The studies for both untitled, 2006–07, and untitled, 2007, capture the spontaneity of Shapiro's hand-held, inventive process (I will return to issues raised by studies of this kind).

The exceptional flexibility of the angular joints—a flexibility facilitated by the use of wire, cord, and a pin gun as devices for rapidly linking the elements—contributes a particularly organic feel to the lengths of material. The subsequent mapping and engineering is designed to retain as much of the complexity of the junctures as possible, whether in the form of a large-scale assemblage of units of wood (which are themselves boxlike constructions of separate wood panels) or in cast elements of metal (which, as indicated, often bear wood-textured surfaces). Shapiro's irregular angles and skewed connections dissociate his sculptural objects from the orthogonal regularity of typical architectural spaces. Although he had set much of his early work directly on the floor—see *One Hand Forming*, 1971 (fig. 6)—his resistance to architecture led him away from most of his Minimalist contemporaries, especially Carl Andre (see *Steel Zinc Plain*, 1969; fig. 7): "I think the way an Andre hugs the floor is … a brilliant idea, but it's not really about assertion. It's about capitulation." Andre, in other words, had surrendered the sculptural object to the spatial logic of the architectural environment. To the contrary, Shapiro realized that to externalize his emotion, "the work had to really depart—had to break away—from the space that it was in and not be determined by the space itself."[13] The clay forms of *One Hand Forming* used the floor merely as a location of display, not as a point of reference. The action of the work was hand action, which had little to do with issues of weight and counterweight or volume and container. Shapiro has been consistent in wanting his transient feelings to prevail—as if his work were being handled in the ambient air and subject to turning this way or that, without suffering disabling structural consequences. Whereas Andre's floor pieces relate to the architectural ground plane at every point and raise no engineering issues, Shapiro's works often avoid contact with the floor to the greatest extent possible, challenging gravity to do something about it. In this, too, he has been consistent. Untitled, 2005–06 (pp. 16–17) and untitled, 2006–07 (fig. 8), each rest on three tenuous points, the structural minimum.[14]

Animation

As he creates his airy models, Shapiro's complex articulation of joints appears no less alive than he is. This is the source of his sculptural figuration. As we know, he once referred to the condition of an artist's work as "implied figuration." The modifier is probably unnecessary: implied figuration *is* figuration; marking, shaping, forming *is* figuration. Shapiro's sculptures figure movement: they imply bending, twisting, and pivoting at the angled joints. His structural articulation

fig. 6:
One Hand Forming, 1971
fired clay, 77 units, 1 1/2" diameter x 3 1/2" each; 9 x 34 x 4" overall, installed

fig. 7:
Carl Andre
Steel Zinc Plain, 1969, steel and zinc plates, 3/8 x 72 1/2 x 72 1/2"
Tate Gallery, London

fig. 8:
untitled, 2006–07, wood, oil, and casein, 32 1/2 x 40 x 29", unique

fig. 9:
untitled, 1983–84, bronze, 80 3/4 x 80 x 52"

fig. 10:
untitled, 1997–98, white bronze, 17 1/8 x 13 1/2 x 21 1/4", unique

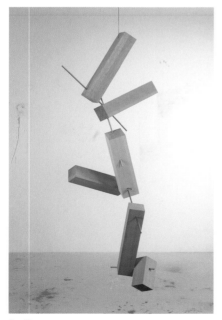

fig. 11:
untitled, 1998, wood and steel, 79 x 58 x 30"

generates qualities associated with animation, the life force. Here my verb *associated* may be the natural term to use but is too much of a conceptual abstraction, too rational a notion. We sense the factor of animation more immediately than by association—intuitively—without need of a process of mental comparison (representation) or logical deduction (abstraction). It is as if each of Shapiro's configurations of wood or bronze became self-activating as quickly as the sculptor's hand attached its component parts: "You're just sticking it together. ... Language is never as concise as art."[15] Shapiro's art succeeds in its own terms to the extent that the spontaneity of "just sticking it together" remains throughout the sometimes lengthy process of conversion from small model to full-scale construction.

Building the sculptures at full scale, an obvious problem arises. No matter how airy, the works are also weighty and require a means of support for purposes of display. Perhaps previously excluded, architecture now re-enters the sculptural picture. There are a number of possibilities. When at least three elements make contact with the support surface, a work can stand around its center of gravity: this principle applies to two works already mentioned, untitled, 2005–06 and untitled, 2006–07. When the form is such that contact with the support is still more limited, a work can be cantilevered, anchored to a floor or wall: untitled, 1983–84 (fig. 9), and untitled, 1997–98 (fig. 10), are examples, each dynamic enough to suggest that the anchor does not restrain it. Or a work can hang by a wire from a surface above: untitled, 1998 (fig. 11), is suspended in this way, with metal rods used to produce a rigid configuration of its separate, dynamically angled elements, which, empathetically, hardly *feel* rigid.

In every instance, Shapiro's sculpture draws its animating energy not from its grounding or means of support, nor from the volume of architectural space that may surround it, but from its internal tensions. Like a motile organism, each work extends from and revolves around an internal center of gravity. The cantilevered "figure" of untitled, 1997–98, looks as if it could move laterally along its wall as well as extending its reach outward, perpendicular to the wall. The effect does not merely stem from the sculpture's vague resemblance to a human body striding, but from the swiveling and twisting motions implied by the tenuously angled connections of the elements. Movement and animation become figured features, hardly in need of a humanoid body. In this respect, the work becomes a self-regulating automaton, within which we imagine a secreted soul—the motivating source of the physical movement that is, we realize, the object's own potential. Rather than representing or abstracting the life of another object or body, it figures animation as its own property.

Untitled, 2002–07 (pp. 30–31) evokes a body with a soul, yet bears no appreciable visual likeness to a human body—certainly far less likeness than we perceive in untitled, 1997–98. This expansive figuration in bronze nevertheless evokes the *feel* of the body. It elicits feelings of living in a body by exemplifying the strain, stretch, reach, and general sense of effort we experience kinesthetically, viscerally, and psychologically (recall Shapiro's allusion to "the psychology of the form"). Human effort appears in many guises. Shapiro notes how difficult it was to engineer the balance and stability of this configuration while retaining the "original sense of fragility" in the corresponding maquette. One end of the structure is relatively massive and seems to anchor the remainder, yet it exhibits a certain looseness and implied flexibility. The other end cantilevers so dramatically that it might appear to dissolve into the air. The sculpture speaks to the human fascination with driving body and mind to their respective limits. Tracing the elements of this work through its articulated joints and out to its extremities produces at once exhilaration and pain, the two sensations that in combination indicate an extreme of human effort. This sculpture avoids being "colossal" despite its size—approximately 28 feet in width and about 13 feet in both height and depth—because its configuration allows the viewer to focus on the play of separate elements in virtual movement. The various prismatic forms seem to bend, pivot, twist, and slip at their joints. Shapiro gave the separate surfaces a variety of curving, saw-cut textures, transferred to the bronze from wooden patterns. The curves contrast with the blocky form of each individually cast element—a surface effect that, like the play of the joints, introduces a humanizing tactile sense to this larger-than-life structure. As heavy as untitled, 2002–07 is, it rests on only three points, as if preparing to rise.

Emotional images

The feelings that the happiness or misfortune of a real person may cause us to experience arise only through the mediation of an image of these states. The ingeniousness of the first novelist lay in grasping that the image was itself the sole element essential to emotional processing, and that the simplification of removing real individuals from consideration would decidedly improve the process.
— Marcel Proust, 1913 [16]

Shapiro's sculptures generate emotion-inducing images like those we encounter through novels, a parallel form of figuration. Fictions or figured things expand people's consciousness, the range of their feelings, and their awareness of their feelings. Marcel Proust understood that the imagery he derived from reading provided him with a broader range of experience than the life he actually lived. From this fact of life, he theorized that a figured image—whether generated by a text, a photograph, a painting, or a sculpture—would induce the most intense emotional response. It would have the potential to introduce new emotions to a reader's or viewer's experience—emotions free of reductive classification—emotions that you feel but cannot name.

Modern critics have sometimes valued visual art for providing this nameless quality of emotional experience: "You can't specify what the emotion is but are profoundly stirred nevertheless." [17] This was Clement Greenberg's comment on Willem de Kooning's early abstractions (which derive from, and may well have incorporated, his early representations). In Shapiro's case, emotionally charged images emerge from the three dimensions of sculpture within the immediacy of a working process: "It's anti-planning. I take an element and I add or subtract it (to or from the existing configuration). It's a way of working ... with contingency. ... The volume extends you, it's an extension of yourself. ... I like injecting life into the inanimate: using…wood to express life." [18] From early in his career, Shapiro used his creative practice to lead him to qualities he felt he had not yet "gotten in touch with"; by engaging a diverse set of materials and processes for creating art, he would "force" himself to confront a range of unfamiliar, disorienting, and perhaps discomforting feelings. [19] "I find out what I want as I go along." [20]

To find something unknown about yourself or in yourself, including feelings never felt before: this is not an unusual claim on the part of a modern artist, yet the words conceal a strange realization. We find our desires, our wants, and their attendant emotional states as we move through experience. We feel our conscious desires after the fact, as we sense that our actions either satisfy or fail them. Perhaps only when we fail desire do we truly realize desire, for otherwise it has no cause to surface. What you "want" is what you lack in order to be emotionally fulfilled—a need that will never be satisfied fully. To find the ultimate aesthetic and emotional satisfaction would amount to creative death, loss of the need for further creativity, a spiritual death if not an organic one. Better to remain dissatisfied, at least for an artist with ambition, such as Shapiro: "I think all the reachings in my work (are about) not being content with the way I am, and needing more experience and a greater richness in order to work."[21] Yes: "I find out what I want as I go along."

Emotions mature and ripen through experience of the type of aesthetically isolated imagery to which Proust alluded. This imagery is likely to affect individuals without their understanding why. Nothing need be said about it, except when attempting to meet the demands of critical reason. Reason itself requires a verbal supplement, as if the mental image generated by material form (even by a text) were in need of a second mental image, derived from verbal commentary and interpretation. On numerous occasions, Shapiro has answered the needs of reason by speaking freely and skillfully of his sculptural practice, addressing with words the aesthetic and expressive issues he explores visually. For the catalogue of his retrospective at the Whitney Museum of American Art in 1982, to take one example, he supplied extensive commentary, moving from a description of his works to speculation on the aesthetic and phenomenological issues that, on reflection, proved to have been at stake in his sculptural production.

In the Whitney catalogue, Shapiro's discussion of untitled, 1973–74 (fig. 12)—a cast iron figure of a simple, generic chair, only 3 inches in its greatest dimension—ends with a distinction between size and scale. The small size of this type of work was so thoroughly unconventional at the time that viewers could not accept it without question. Shapiro took responsibility for answering for his work. He suggested that size is objectively absolute and disembodied, whereas scale is embodied and subjectively experiential. His chair had scale, which was what it required. "I thought there was no need

to make it any bigger," he stated, invoking a pragmatic economy: "The scale of a piece is its viability in that size, not the size itself." To grasp the import of Shapiro's distinction, we need to think in terms of feelings, as he did then and still does. At times, the sense of scale, which ought to be subjective, may seem to be as objective as a measurement of size. This is an aspect of what Shapiro called the "viability" of his small sculpture, the very general sense of its meaningfulness; we share this sense because human experience tends to agree on how bodies feel in relation to things—experientially, to anyone who inhabits a human body, which is every one of us. The logic of Shapiro's explanation is inductive; he abstracts from everyday kinesthetic experience, realizing a general connection between bodies and things. In this instance, the crucial link is the right-angled form shared by chairs and the bodies that sit in them: "I described the right-angled space of the seat of a chair, and that is the familiar space of a chair—the space one occupies. ... We know that space. ... Our bodies and our experience become condensed." He meant that the abstract form of a chair, no matter what its size, condenses the experience of the body and the experience of a (real) chair. Shapiro concluded that his sculpted chair "evokes physical memory," a powerful reserve of sensation independent of the size of any particular object.[22] Like a dream or an emotion or even a mere color, a memory has no size, but rather scale. The small size of the chair does not prevent a viewer from relating to it in terms of timeless memory as opposed to immediate use (none in this case, because of the size). Shapiro's chair functioned as an emotional image, "the sole element essential to emotional processing" (as Proust would have wanted it).

Kick away

> I want to kick away within my own sort of perspective.
> And that's essentially what gives the work a kind of
> touch and a kind of edge, and a sadness.
> — Joel Shapiro, 1975[23]

As a writer, I naturally respect the chosen words of an artist, the most knowledgeable person to offer comment. But I also remain wary of regarding artists' descriptions and statements of purpose too literally, for an artist's range of expression is as limited by prevailing uses of language as a critic's is. Shapiro knows that his words and the objects he creates are incommensurables. As intelligent as his mini-theory of size and scale may be, these terms and their logic do no more than glance over the surface of qualities to be sensed in the objects he creates, and they only approximate the connection

fig. 12:
untitled, 1973–74, cast iron, 3 x 1 1/4 x 1 3/4"

to human feeling. Shapiro's language amounts to a generalizing theory applied to an art—his own—that is far too particular to be captured by it.

At times, an artist's words may seem to leave reason and theory behind, functioning to induce emotion, like a work of art. Here, too, we should not assume that the two forms of expression, the visual and the verbal, run parallel. Shapiro warns that his emotional state during the creation of a work may not transfer to the finished work as its meaning. "I'm sure when I made these pieces"—he was referring to early works of around 1973 to 1976—"I was angry and demanding, although the emotional means of generating a piece and how the piece functions in the world should not be confused."[24]

We should consider the emotive force of an artist's words only very generally, then; and the judgment is likely to be quite subjective. Exercising my own subjectivity, I was struck by a passage in an interview Shapiro gave in 1975, which seemed particularly revealing to me. Here he used the verb *kick away*, apparently quite spontaneously. It is casual, colloquial language, yet quite a strong metaphor. Kicking away suggests determination but also deprecation and rejection. Shapiro seemed to be referring to rejecting or jettisoning something in himself. The sense of self-rejection, as well as the self-transcendence that often follows it, would correspond to his warning not to equate his specific range of feeling at a certain moment to the feeling that might be associated with the corresponding work. A work kicked away is not necessarily a work rejected as inferior or as a failure. With every "kick away," the work, to the contrary, might grow exponentially more expressive.

To "kick away within my own sort of perspective" has a certain ring to it, at least to me; the phrasing seems to belong to the time it was uttered. I wonder whether Shapiro had been alluding, albeit indirectly, to the work of Ludwig Wittgenstein. During the late 1960s and early 1970s, Wittgenstein's writings were inspiring not only academics but artists. It was often said (in so many words) that Wittgenstein had "kicked away" the ladder of his own analytical investigation of language, realizing that poetry was the only solution to philosophical problems—not an unfavorable conclusion for visual artists who had chosen a "poetic" route from the start.

The penultimate passage from Wittgenstein's *Tractatus Logico-Philosophicus* reads: "Anyone who understands me eventually recognizes (my propositions) as nonsensical, when he has used them—as steps—to climb up beyond them. (He must, so to speak, throw away the ladder after he has climbed up.)"[25] The German term for *throw away* is *wegwerfen*; *kick away* is a suitable substitute in colloquial English, if only because the image of climbing up makes it at least as logical that a foot, rather than a hand, would act to "throw away" the supportive ladder. A person who "kicks away" at his own perspective—deprecating his own position even as it emerges—is someone driven to exceed himself. During the 1970s, Shapiro often referred to the strength of his ambition, and three decades later he still does. Notoriously, Wittgenstein was dissatisfied with himself and his work. After his *Tractatus*, he shifted his intellectual direction radically, and there were periods when he abandoned philosophy to pursue other occupations (architect, school teacher). Although Shapiro has never abandoned sculpture, kicking away internally, "within my own perspective," suggests the quirky extremes of his creative process, often marked by radical turns and reversals: producing a study but then inverting the form; painting a sculpture but then removing the color; configuring, disfiguring, configuring again. Here is his account from 1995: "Chop off parts, rip the form apart, and reassemble. It is an open process. I can change the facts."[26] Kick away the old facts and create new ones.

By 1975, the time of the "kick away" statement, Shapiro was already a mature artist with reason to be satisfied with what he had achieved. But he has always been restless. If I take his statement at face value, his kicking away was exposing three inherent qualities of his art that it seems he was prepared to accept and maintain: its "touch," its "edge," and its "sadness." Why these words or concepts rather than others? I asked him, but he no longer recalls specific reasons for his having chosen touch, edge, and sadness.

Touch (movement)

> The painter or sculptor ... depicts the transition from one pose to another. He indicates how the first imperceptibly slips into being the second. In his work you detect a part of what has been as you discover part of what will be.
> — Auguste Rodin, 1910[27]

> Sculpture sums up bodily movement.
> — Joel Shapiro, 2005[28]

Touch, edge, sadness: the first of these objects of conceptual focus—touch, the sense of touch, the act of touch, the reciprocity we understand as touching and being touched—all

fig. 13:
untitled, 2006–07, wood, 75 3/4 x 78 x 48", unique

this involves movement. As a way of assessing a form in space, we move the hand to differentiate those qualities accessible to the sense of touch: for example, extension but not brightness, texture but not color. Touch moves. It is itself animated and animating. By transferring its momentum, it lends life to things. We perceive the active handling of materials, the contact that is the artist's touch, in the characteristically abrupt joining of elements in Shapiro's sculptures—at once casual and deliberate in effect. Untitled, 2007 (p. 19) consists of six attached elements, four of which seem to relate to the gravitational pull of the ground, while two become decidedly vertical and appear ready to lift. The verticality causes this composition of forms to appear figural or totemic. Its touch is certainly not easy to describe—almost painful. I say this because of the extreme tenuousness of the crucial points of contact—the limited areas where the upper shaftlike element establishes contact with the supportive blocks below. From certain angles untitled, 2007, gives a very stable impression, while from others it seems about to break apart: configure and disfigure, as Shapiro might say. Along these lines, he recently stated his interest in "instability, imbalance."[29] Imbalance shows in a work like untitled, 2006–07 (fig. 13), where one element within a group of several supported by a central shaft is surprisingly elongated, extending downward beyond the point that a conventional sense of proportion would allow. This type of imbalance—no, not really imbalance, for the work is not collapsing—this "imbalance," seems to bring a second sense of touch the

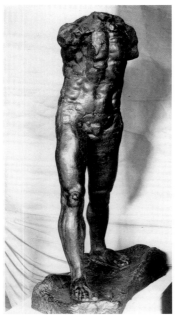

fig. 14:
Auguste Rodin
Walking man (L'homme qui marche), 1877
bronze, 84 x 28 1/4 x 61 5/8"
Musée Rodin, Paris

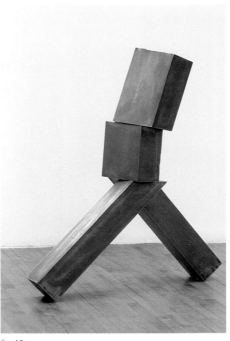

fig. 15:
untitled, 1987, bronze, 49 1/2 x 15 1/4 x 44 1/4"

first. A way to understand a sculpture characterized by instability and imbalance is to realize that more than one movement is being incorporated within the structure. Think of its several views not as photographic stills but as frames of a film that must be compressed into a moment—a summing up, as Shapiro might say (compressing feeling as well as "bodily movement").

This is what Rodin had also achieved, although perhaps less challengingly, since he set his multiple movements within clearly representational bodies (see *Walking Man*, 1877; fig. 14). The commentary on Rodin by the phenomenologist Maurice Merleau-Ponty now reads as if he were describing a typical work of Shapiro: "Movement is given, says Rodin, by an image in which the arms, the legs, the trunk, and the head are each taken at a different instant, (to portray) the body in an attitude which it never at any instant really held and which imposes fictive linkages between the parts, as if this mutual confrontation of incompossibles could, and could alone, cause transition and duration to arise in bronze."[30] By this description, Rodin was not representing, but figuring. If he represented anything, it was the feel of the body, not the appearance of the body, at least not the conventional, pictorial, camera-view sense of the body: "It is photography that lies," he proclaimed, as he argued for the special function of sculpture.[31]

At times, Shapiro has been very explicit about his desire to incorporate conflicting movement within an animated form, which does nothing but enhance the movement, as if kicking it away to a higher place. Untitled, 1987 (fig. 15) amounts to his own walking man: "I wanted a piece that moved both backward and forward simultaneously. So, I ended up cutting the torso and reversing it."[32] In a similar manner, his cantilevered form of 1983–84 "appears to configure up and down simultaneously, so that arms read as legs and vice versa" (see fig. 9).[33] The sculpture inverts, reverts, or merely turns. In the language of figuration, to figure an image is to turn it, to move it into another form.[34]

Edge (pin gun)

> Regarding inverting the form or the image: ... the same form, depending on the orientation, changes meaning.
> — Joel Shapiro, 2007[35]

What gives a sculpture its edge? In Shapiro's case, it is the combination of immediacy and tentativeness in works that sometimes become quite large. This tentativeness is the mirror side of the "incompossibility" to which Merleau-Ponty alluded—the capacity for a work to move in two directions at once, or simply keep moving, even when immobile. Shapiro's concern for edgy movement is evident in his study technique, for which he uses any number of impermanent fastening devices to manipulate and combine elements with the greatest rapidity: wire, cord, glue, a pin gun. This last is a device that shoots small metal pins into wood and other rigid materials, similar to the action of a staple gun; but because the pins are straight, when two elements are fastened, they can easily be pulled back apart by hand, twisted, or merely loosened (see the detail of the study for untitled, 2006–07; fig. 16). Such actions quickly create a great variety of angular joints. Eventually transferred to works of much larger scale, the configuration of the joints preserves the initial emotional spontaneity associated with the emergence of the form.

Because Shapiro's studies are quite small, he can adjust them while holding them in a hand in the air (as I've mentioned). Holding a study in this manner, he can easily rotate or invert it. Gravity hardly concerns him, or only negatively ("I'm interested in the dislocation of the body from the ground").[36] His surprising variety of form results in part from the liberties he takes in radically altering the orientation of a study. In at least one case, he inverted a study at a relatively late stage in the development of the work—untitled, 2002–03 (fig. 17, p. 14). Once he had adjusted the full-scale structure accordingly, its engineering required the use of a metal rod to support an element extending far into the lateral air. "I flipped the model over and then flipped the piece over," he says; "I just felt that the piece had much more life in this inverted state. … Sculpture is … a construct.

fig. 16:
Detail of a study for untitled, 2006–07 (pp. 24–25), showing how the pin gun works as a fastening device.

fig. 17:
untitled, 2002–03, wood and steel, 7' 9" x 12' 5" x 9' 2"

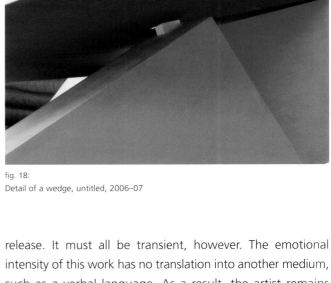

fig. 18:
Detail of a wedge, untitled, 2006–07

It's not part of the natural world." In other words, sculpture has its own internal animation; its uprightness is a contingent factor, not an essential one. To maintain the stability and rigidity of movemented, incompossible constructions, a sculptor has to apply ingenuity; hence, the variety of wedges, brackets, pins, and rods that become visual bonuses in the array of forms that compose Shapiro's works. The rod and bracket in untitled, 2002–03, is the distant cousin of, say, the wedges to be found at the angles of untitled, 2006–07 (see the detail of a wedge [fig. 18], and compare pp. 28–29). The wedge not only stabilizes the structure but also provides added incident. It introduces another kind of articulation, which, like the power-saw patterns in the cast bronzes and the irregularly water-blasted paint surfaces of works in wood (see untitled, 2005–07; p. 27), aids in establishing human scale—a human presence on the edge.

Sadness (pending)

> It's hard to match the level of immediacy and abruptness of a drawing in a sculpture. (But) I can make a model, a small model, with my hands ... I can put something together with my hands.
> — Joel Shapiro, 1996 [37]

Why would sculpture be associated with sadness? It may be that sadness must accompany elation. The hand-oriented work in which Shapiro absorbs himself is deeply fulfilling, even at moments of temporary frustration (the absence of a tool or material, an interruption, a lapse of attention). His process of making studies for larger works entails remarkable expressive freedom and a satisfying emotional release. It must all be transient, however. The emotional intensity of this work has no translation into another medium, such as a verbal language. As a result, the artist remains isolated with his work for as long as he works. The isolation is compounded by Shapiro's tendency to kick away the "ladder" (the learning curve) of each study and propel himself into yet another insecure situation. Whatever moments of accomplishment arise can only be enjoyed if they are— sadly—very short-lived. "All that he would otherwise have loved and admired seemed to him to be shorn of its worth by the transience which was its doom." [38] The pain of transience, even if self-induced, has no remedy other than finding distraction in another round of transiency. Certain artists never stop working.

This aesthetic sadness is not so sad. Perhaps the bittersweetness of poignancy would be a better designation. *Poignant* connotes pleasure as well as pain—in effect, a movement of the emotions, an emotional incompossibility that causes the bearer of the emotions to be all the more enriched in a specifically human capacity. With Shapiro's work, poignancy shows in the way that the individual elements of a composition tend to be very similar yet act very differently. Some are supportive, while others are supported. The sculptures demonstrate the tentativeness of human action. If Shapiro were to invert or rotate a particular form—as he may well have done when studying its hand-held maquette— then the supported might become the supporting. The place of each element is pending—hanging in the "imbalance" that is Shapiro's concern. Look at the dense structures of untitled, 2005–06 (pp. 16–17), untitled, 2006–07 (p. 21), untitled, 2006 (p. 20), and the somewhat simpler untitled, 2006–07 (fig. 8). Determine which elements are supporting and which, to the contrary, are hanging from those elements, pending. Some of the answers do not come quickly, especially because certain pairs of elements will be virtually identical save for their contingent relationship to each other. It is easy to imagine a turn of sculptural fortune this way or that, resulting in a different tectonic configuration. The work would remain the same sculptural being with the same material soul set in its internal center. But its animation and emotional force would have changed. All in life is pending. A corpus of sculptural work that leads to this thought—to this emotion—is worth a critic's best efforts at discrimination.

Notes

1. For example, Donald Kuspit describes the character of Shapiro's work in terms of subverting a number of standard oppositions, including, ultimately, the opposition of self and other: "Shapiro's sculptures are abstract 'inventions' with a human identity, and their dialectical core—the ambiguously resolved relationship between their parts, and their overall split, self-subverting character—is human as well as formal in import"; Donald Kuspit, "Joel Shapiro's Figurative Constructions," in Hubertus Gassner, ed., *Joel Shapiro: Skulpturen 1993–1997*, exh. cat. (Munich: Haus der Kunst, 1998), p. 60. To facilitate research for this essay, Joel Shapiro generously offered me access to his studio, to works in progress, and to archival material; he was equally generous in replying to queries on details of his practice. I am indebted to him as well as to Douglas Baxter and PaceWildenstein Gallery for their essential aid. Special thanks go to Caitlin Haskell for valuable research assistance in Austin. Unless otherwise noted, opinions and quoted statements attributed to Joel Shapiro derive from conversations and email exchanges that occurred between February and October 2007.

2. Shapiro, statement (January 2 and 3, 1990), in Deborah Leveton, "Interview," in Julia Brown Turrell, ed., *Joel Shapiro: Tracing the Figure*, exh. cat. (Des Moines: Des Moines Art Center, 1990), p. 56.

3. Shapiro, in Leveton, "Interview," p. 46.

4. Over the years, Shapiro seems to have relied increasingly on the concept of figuration as a way of explaining himself; this may be a result of his realization that the opposition of representation and abstraction excluded too much of the reality of a middle position. For example, in an interview of 1979, he stated: "I don't think (there) are purely abstract pieces. ... I think all pieces are essentially the metaphors for thought"; Shapiro, statement in John Coplans, "Joel Shapiro: An Interview," *Akron Art Institute: Dialogue* (January–February 1979), p. 9. "Metaphors for thought" would be synonymous with "figures for thought."

5. Shapiro, statement (April 12, 1990) in "Interview: Joel Shapiro Talks with Paul Cummings," *Drawing* 12 (July–August 1990), p. 33. See also Shapiro, in Leveton, "Interview," p. 55: "Maybe sculpture is less abstract than painting because it exists in real space."

6. Shapiro, in Leveton, "Interview," p. 46.

7. Shapiro, "Commentaries," in Richard Marshall, ed., *Joel Shapiro*, exh. cat. (New York: Whitney Museum of American Art, 1982), p. 101.

8. Shapiro, interview conducted by Kate Horsfield and Lyn Blumenthal for Video Data Bank, Art Institute of Chicago, transcript, 1984 (courtesy Joel Shapiro).

9. Klaus Kertess, "Dancing with Gravity," *Joel Shapiro: New Wood and Bronze Sculpture*, exh. cat. (New York: PaceWildenstein, 1998), p. 7.

10. Shapiro, "Joel Shapiro: In Conversation" (interview by Jock Reynolds), in Jock Reynolds, ed., *Joel Shapiro: Sculpture in Clay, Plaster, Wood, Iron, and Bronze, 1971–1997*, exh. cat. (Andover: Addison Gallery of American Art, 1998), p. 71. For Shapiro, the "body" is usually at once male and female and can at times be a vertebrate animal body, say, a dog or a horse. "There are a couple of pieces that have breasts (but) if the work is abstract enough I think it gets away from that male/femaleness"; Shapiro, in Leveton, "Interview," p. 56.

11. Shapiro, in Leveton, "Interview," p. 66.

12. Shapiro, "Joel Shapiro: In Conversation," p. 86. For sculptures at full scale, it would be nearly impossible to find lengths of milled wood structurally, visually, and dimensionally perfect enough to use, so Shapiro builds individual elements from separate panels cut to form elongated, hollow boxes.

13. Shapiro, oral history interview by Lewis Kachur, October 26, 1988, Archives of American Art, Smithsonian Institution, transcript (courtesy Joel Shapiro).

14. There are exceptions: Shapiro continues to create the occasional work in plaster or bronze designed to lie flat on the floor; but such works are irregularly shaped, can be placed anywhere, and are readily perceived as independent of their surroundings.

15. Shapiro, in Leveton, "Interview," pp. 56, 66. Shapiro's point has a remote source in Kantian aesthetics, in the notion that acts of creativity do not lend themselves to causal self-analysis; the artist "does not himself know how the ideas ... have entered into his head"; Immanuel Kant, *The Critique of Judgment* (1790), trans. James Creed Meredith (Oxford: Oxford University Press, 1952), p. 308. To Kant, Shapiro adds a Freudian nuance: "When you're working, everything you're thinking about is like an externalization of repressed thinking"; Shapiro, "Interview with the Artist" (interview by Claire Lilley), in Claire Lilley, ed., *Joel Shapiro: Sculpture 1974–1999*, exh. cat. (Wakefield: Yorkshire Sculpture Park, 1999), 24.

16. Marcel Proust, *A la recherche du temps perdu: Du côté de chez Swann* (1913), 2 vols. (Paris: Gallimard, 1954 [1913]), vol. 1, p. 115 (my translation).

17. Clement Greenberg, in Russell W. Davenport, ed., "A *Life* Round Table on Modern Art," *Life* (October 11, 1948), p. 62.

18. Shapiro, statement in Thierry Dufrène, "Interview with Joel Shapiro," in Thierry Dufrène, ed., *Correspondances: Joel Shapiro / Jean-Baptiste Carpeaux*, exh. cat. (Paris: Musée d'Orsay, 2005), pp. 28, 32.

19. Shapiro, statement (February 6, 1975) in Liza Bear, "Joel Shapiro Torquing," *Avalanche* (Summer 1975), p. 17.

20. Shapiro, in Dufrène, *Correspondances*, p. 32.

21. Shapiro, interview conducted by Liza Bear, second take, February 9, 1975, unedited typescript with manuscript edits (courtesy Joel Shapiro).

22. Shapiro, "Commentaries," p. 96.

23. Shapiro, in Bear, "Joel Shapiro Torquing," p. 17.

24. Shapiro, "Commentaries," p. 98. In an early review, Jeremy Gilbert-Rolfe alluded to the difference between Shapiro's personal expression and the viewer's response, arguing that the artist's sculpture of a chair could be "about projection—projection, on the part of the viewer, into the space of the work," even as it originated in "extremely personal ... autobiographical connections"; Jeremy Gilbert-Rolfe, "Joel Shapiro: Works in Progress," *Artforum* 12 (December 1973), p. 74.

25. Ludwig Wittgenstein, *Tractatus Logico-Philosophicus* (1921), trans. D. F. Pears and B. F. McGuinness (London: Routledge and Kegan Paul, 1971), p. 151. When Stanley Fish published *Self-Consuming Artifacts* in 1972, he used the throwing-away statement as an epigraph to his entire argument. Reviewing Fish's book, Quentin Skinner converted the phrase into "kick(ing) away the ladder by which he has ascended"—a natural substitution. See Stanley E. Fish, *Self-Consuming Artifacts* (Berkeley: University of California Press, 1972), p. i; Quentin Skinner, "Self-Consuming Artifacts," *Modern Philology* 72 (1974), p. 93.

26. Shapiro, statement to Ellen Phelan, in Amy Newman, ed., *Joel Shapiro: Painted Wood Sculpture and Drawings*, exh. cat. (New York: PaceWildenstein, 1995), p. 11.

27. Auguste Rodin, *L'art*, Paul Gsell, ed. (Paris: Bernard Grasset, 1911), pp. 76–77 (my translation). Gsell published a number of these same statements in 1910, presumably the year that his conversations with Rodin occurred.

28. Shapiro, in Dufrène, *Correspondances*, p. 24.

29. Ibid., p. 26.

30. Maurice Merleau-Ponty, "Eye and Mind" (1961), in James M. Edie, ed., *The Primacy of Perception*, trans. Carlton Dallery (Evanston: Northwestern University Press, 1964), p. 185.

31. Rodin, *L'art*, p. 86 (my translation).

32. Shapiro, in Leveton, "Interview," p. 66.

33. Ibid., p. 58.

34. A figure is a trope is a turn. One turn deserves, produces, another.

35. Shapiro, statement to the author, August 21, 2007.

36. Shapiro, in Leveton, "Interview," p. 60.

37. Shapiro, statement in James Cuno, "Joel Shapiro on His Recent Prints: An Interview," *Print Collector's Newsletter* 27 (May–June 1996), p. 50.

38. Sigmund Freud, "On Transience" (1916 [1915]), in James Strachey, ed. and trans., *The Standard Edition of the Complete Psychological Works of Sigmund Freud*, vol. 14 (London: Hogarth Press, 1986), p. 305.

untitled | 2005–2006, bronze, 36 7/8 x 37 7/8 x 24 3/4", edition 1/3

untitled | 2007, bronze, 9' 4" x 4' 7 7/8" x 2' 11 1/2", edition 1/3

untitled | 2006, wood and casein, 37 1/4 x 28 1/2 x 21 1/4", unique

untitled | 2006–2007, bronze, 64 5/8 x 50 7/8 x 48 1/4", edition 1/3

untitled | 2007, bronze, 57 $^3/_8$ x 41 $^1/_8$ x 25 $^7/_8$", edition 1/3

untitled | 2006–2007, wood and casein, 5' 1/2" x 9' 3" x 5' 1/2", unique

untitled | 2005–2007, wood and casein, 47 1/4 x 53 1/8 x 39 3/4", unique

untitled | 2006–2007, wood, casein, and oil, 83 ¹/₂ x 83 ¹/₄ x 64 ¹/₄", unique

untitled | 2002–2007, bronze, 13' 4" x 27' 9 1/2" x 12' 11", edition 1/2

CHECKLIST

16–17   untitled | 2005–2006   bronze, 36 $^7/_8$ x 37 $^7/_8$ x 24 $^3/_4$", edition 1/3

19   untitled | 2007   bronze, 9' 4" x 4' 7 $^7/_8$" x 2' 11 $^1/_2$", edition 1/3

20   untitled | 2006   wood and casein, 37 $^1/_4$ x 28 $^1/_2$ x 21 $^1/_4$", unique

21   untitled | 2006–2007   bronze, 64 $^5/_8$ x 50 $^7/_8$ x 48 $^1/_4$", edition 1/3

23   untitled | 2007   bronze, 57 $^3/_4$ x 41 $^1/_8$ x 25 $^7/_8$", edition 1/3

24–25   untitled | 2006–2007   wood and casein, 5' $^1/_2$" x 9' 3" x 5' $^1/_2$", unique

27   untitled | 2005–2007   wood and casein, 47 $^1/_4$ x 53 $^1/_8$ x 39 $^3/_4$", unique

28–29   untitled | 2006–2007   wood, casein, and oil, 83 $^1/_2$ x 83 $^1/_4$ x 64 $^1/_4$", unique

30–31   untitled | 2002–2007   bronze, 13' 4" x 27' 9 $^1/_2$" x 12' 11", edition 1/2

Cover: untitled, 2002–2007 (detail)
Pages 3–4: untitled 2005–2007 (detail)

Photography:
Courtesy the artist; pp. 6 (figs. 2, 3, 5), 7 (fig. 6), p. 10 (fig. 12), 13, 14 (fig. 18), 24
Courtesy Paula Cooper Gallery, New York; pp. 5, 12 (fig. 15)
Ken Burris Studio; p. 8 (fig. 11)
Foto Marburg /Art Resource, NY; p. 12 (fig. 14)
Ellen Labenski; p. 2, p. 7 (fig. 8), 19, 20, 25, 27–29
Ellen Labenski and Joerg Lohse; 21
Ellen Labenski and Colin White; cover, pp. 30–31
Kerry Ryan McFate; 23
Kerry Ryan McFate and Joerg Lohse; p. 12 (fig. 13), 16–17
Tate, London, Art Resource, NY; p. 7 (fig. 7)
Jonty Wilde; p. 8 (fig. 9)
Ellen Page Wilson; p. 8 (fig. 10), p. 14 (fig. 17)

Design:
Tomo Makiura

Production:
Paul Pollard, Tucker Capparell

Color correction:
Motohiko Tokuta

Printing:
Meridian Printing, East Greenwich, Rhode Island

ISBN: 978-1-930743-81-6